YOGA PSYCHOLOGY
Understanding and Awakening Kundalini

Dedicated to
Shrii Shrii A'nandamurti Baba

By **Maetreyii Ma Nolan Ph.D.**

Copyright © 2015 by Maetreyii Ma, M. E. Nolan Ph.D.
All rights reserved. No part of this book may be
reproduced, scanned,
or distributed in any printed or electronic form without
permission.
Printed in the United States of America
ISBN: **978-0-9863047-7-4**

About the Writings

The contents of this book are from oral teachings inspired by Shrii Shrii Anandamurti or 'Baba' as he is affectionately called. Anandamurti Baba' lived and taught in India from 1921-1990 conveying a diverse body of teachings. Though no longer in physical form, Baba's grace and spiritual presence continues to be the inspiration for these beautiful teachings which come through Maetreyii Ma in the 'Baba Talks'.

Yoga Psychology

For more information on the teachings of
Shrii Shrii Anandamurti
please contact:
Ananda Gurukula Publications
Santa Rosa CA
anandagurukula@gmail.com
707-575-0886

Preface

Additional material to the oral discourses has been added to enhance the readability and to add and clarify relevant content to the original transcripts. A few Sanskrit terms relevant to yogic philosophy and practice are used, as their meaning is more precise in Sanskrit. For the convenience of readers not familiar with these terms, they are defined in a glossary at the end of the book.

Maetreyii Ma

Yoga Psychology

Table of Contents

YOGA PSYCHOLOGY 1
Understanding and Awakening Kundalini 1
About the Writings 1
Preface 3
Table of Contents 5
Introduction 7
Kundalini and the Mind Body Relationship 9
The Psychology of Yoga 25
Transformation of Consciousness and Mind 43
Glands and Sub-glands 53
Nadiis 57
Vrttis of Vishuddha Chakra 59
Awakening Kundalini Safely 67
Vrttis and Spiritual Development 75
Brain Waves and Tonal Waves 81
Subtle Sounds and Language 83
Subtle Sounds and Colors 87
Glossary 89
About the Author and the Origin of These Writings 95

Yoga Psychology

Introduction

This book contains a series of intuitionally received discourses on kundalini and subtle body theory. It delves into the process by which mind interfaces with the physical body and energy and consciousness move. It discusses the rising of kundalini, how mental tendencies of the human mind (vrttis) express, the subtle energy channels (nadiis) through which prana flows, chakras, the role of sound in manifestation, layers of mind and the relationship of these subtle energies to the glandular and nervous systems in the human body.

Through this series of discourses the reader may gain insight into the complex and marvelous system of subtle energy flows which allow the human mind to manifest in a physical body and by which one may come to experience the transformation of consciousness and awakening kundalini.

The text of this book is drawn from oral discourses, and the oral nature of the discourses has been preserved in its editing. A few Sanskrit terms relevant to the discussion of kundalini and subtle body theory are used, as their meaning is most precise in the Sanskrit language. For the convenience of readers not familiar with these terms, they are defined in a glossary at the end of the book.

Yoga Psychology

Kundalini and the Mind Body Relationship

Today's topic will be the relationship between mind and body. There are three things of importance in this area. One is the chakra system, another the mental body, and the third is the physical structure. All of these three bodies come into play for the manifestation of a human being. First I will cover the chakra system.

The kundalini lies coiled at the base of the spine. It is said that it is coiled three times. Three times represents the physical, mental and spiritual realms. This is the life force energy of a human being, not the prana, but the essential essence of their existence. The human mind comes in association with a physical structure and manifests its reactive momentum through the development of the chakras, the plexii and the glands, or propensities as expressed in the body and the nervous system. The glands are developed from the combined expressions of the propensities and the hormonal system regulates these differing expressions. The propensities lie in the outermost layer of the sushumna. The inner most channel, or Brahma nadii, is the fluidal passage of the sleeping serpentine energy of the kundalini. It is through Brahma nadii that the kundalini arises. Surrounding this nadii is another nadii, citrani nadii, in which the fundamental life force takes association with the five fundamental factors. In citrani nadii the kundalini becomes associated with the different factors, and the differing factors will have a multiple of expressions depending upon the degree of pranic energies allotted to them. Surrounding this is the vajra nadii in which the aspects of human experience arise. And surrounding vajra nadii is the plexii or overall arena in which the propensities find physicality.

When desires are physically active, they may be called 'sub-glands'. They are not glands in the physical body; they are activated propensities of the mind through which the pranic force flows. First the desires of the mind come in contact with the basic elements and the biij sounds. From the biij sounds come the sounds of the frequencies (vrtiis). They are not physical sounds, but subtle, psychic tonal frequencies emerging from the arena of the five fundamental factors within citrani nadii. The biij tone breaks apart into the propensities (vrtiis) which constitute the basic tonal avenues of psychic development. When these penetrate out from vajra nadii into the physical body, they move into the arena of the plexii. In this arena they have psycho-physical form. That is to say, they are not glands in the sense that they are physical glands in the body. If you dissect the body you will never find these glands. They are psycho-physical manifestations of the mental propensities. Within the arena of these glands you will find the manifestation of biological factors.

In the plexii and the controlling mandala you will find the development, the correlation of physical development and psychic or mental development. In the plexii the nervous system becomes activated. Within the plexii you will find physical development and glands which correspond to the particular pranic energies which have come through the biij vibratory frequency and have been dispersed into the subtle frequencies of the mental propensities. The propensities – diversified according to the samskaras of the individual – then touch the plexii, which is the nerve interface between the mind and body and developed the mandala complex in a given chakra or center. In this mandala the physical body comes in full association through the nervous system with the subtle body and you have the requisite physical glands. Is it clear?

Q: Usually the nadiis are diagrammed as tubes, sometimes either showing that they intersect the chakras, other times showing a twist at each chakra. In the description you are giving it sounds more as though they are sheaths or layers around the starting point in the center.

The nadiis of which you are speaking are ida and pingala. There are many, many nadiis. Nadii means energy channel. There are many nadiis. Ida and pingala move like this (showing the zig-zag movement). Where ida and pingala intercept you will find the center of the chakra, but within the sushumna, in the subtle body, or the spinal column in the physical body, you will find there are three nadiis. The center most nadii, being Brahma nadii, is the most subtle. The kundalini will rise primarily through Brahma nadii. Around Brahma nadii you have citrani nadii and then vajra nadii. These are sheathes which surround; they are layers within the sushumna.

Q: When ida and pingala intersect, do they intersect once, or do they wind a few times depending on the chakra?

Ida and pingala intersect at each chakra only one time, crossing and changing direction. These are directional nadiis. They will go left or right, one way or another, so that at the chakra they will reverse flows. You see, they reverse [Baba' shows by hands movements the directional change]. They change direction, so this one is going like this in this direction, this one in this direction. They will come to the chakra and they will cross, making a directional shift.

Q: What is the substance of the subtle body? What goes through the nadiis?

The subtle body is composed of life force which is modified in association with a physical structure. Microvita (small life particles) are the energetic components of that life force. What flows through the nadiis is the very subtle psychic flow of mind. It is the inferential flow of mental development or tammatras. You see, the human mind disassociate from physical form or any other vehicle will be an accumulation of reactive momenta, a purely psychic form. When it comes in contact with a physical body, there must be an interface between this mind and the physical structure.

So the mind takes its root in nuladhara chakra. Its

medium for expression is sound. This is not a physical sound, it is a subtle vibratory frequency. It arises from nuladhara chakra. This is the resting place of the unmanifest mind entering the physical body. Mind arises through subtle psychic sounds and moves through the nadiis I have spoken of. This is subtle psychic development. Tanmatra moves, first associating with the biij tones, the five fundamental factors, in citrani nadii and then diversifying according to samskaric development into the propensities (vrttis). For example, in manipura chakra there are ten propensities. A person, due to their development in the past, may have a strong expression in five or six of these, and in four they have little expression. So when the mental flow of their mind comes in contact with the biija sound in the chakra it will cling in, or hold on to, that sound according to sympathetic vibratory frequencies (tammatras), and then it will diversify into the propensities with varying intensities and varying curvatures according to the prior development. When those propensities come in contact with the plexii and the nerves they will begin to resonate in different frequencies, and when the entire mandala is activated, the glandular system of the physical body and the nervous system of the physical body will be regulated according to those samskaric tendencies of the individual mind.

So mind will manifest from the nuladhara chakra, arising through the tonal frequencies until full manifestation has occurred and all of the propensities of the human mind are activated including 'para' and 'apara'. So in this way the human mind enters the physical body and finds psycho-physical parallelism and expression in the physical world. Is it clear?

Q: Could you explain the difference between the terms mandala, plexii and chakra?

Chakra means "focal point". The chakra is the focal point for the subtle body. The chakra is the center or focus for the subtle flow of mind. When it diversifies into psycho-physical expression and activates the nervous system, thus expanding into a broader arena, this is plexii. Plexii are the nerves which are associated with the specific frequencies expressed by the given propensities. In the plexii lie the sub-glands which are the nerve regulators which directly manifest the propensities and influence the physical glandular development. The glandular development and the entire physio-psychic subtle center is all within the mandala formation of that particular energetic vortex. Do you understand? It is very systematic.

Q: Did you say the plexii are the physical nerves?

The plexii bring the subtle tonal frequency in contact with the nervous system within the spinal column and have associated brain functions. So the plexii encompasses the psycho-physical interface between the nervous system and the subtle tonal frequencies. But, you see, it is not quite as you are thinking. There are, within the plexii, sub-glands.

These are psycho-physical interfaces, nerve bundles, but they are called glands because they regulate biochemically. They control biochemical development within the nervous system and in their outer most expression develop the physical glands: the pituitary gland, the pineal gland, the thyroid gland. Is it clear?

Q: What actually happens at the interface between mind and body? Mind seems to be one category of expression of consciousness, but the body is material and very different. How does mind actually affect the expression of body?

Through tonal frequencies, as I have just stated. You see, when there is reactive momenta stored in the mind – in the form of thoughts and ideas which are carried upon inferences – certain mental tendencies may be there. For example, let us say a man did some great harm to another in a past life. He comes in the body and there is latent within his mental expression tremendous guilt. He feels a need to rectify himself for his past action. Though he has no recall of that action the mental propensity of self-recrimination will be there, and this mental tendency of the man will gravitate towards the respective fundamental factor, which is not a lump of clay, it is a tonal wave. At that tonal wave the self-recriminating sentiment will become fixed, and it will shoot out from the central focus in a particular directional flow. So these propensities represent directional flows or desires. It will shoot out in a particular directional flow, and it will take a certain curvature sympathetic to the stored sentiment within the mental structure. Then that will find a biochemical interface in the nervous system of the individual and in the nerve bundles and glandular development. So the development of the glands will in fact be influenced by this past reaction in the mind and certain glands may become under or over developed in specific subtle ways. Certain biochemical configurations will dominate the physiological structure to express this latent samskara. Is it explained?

Q: You spoke of the flow of life force through the sushumna nadii and you said that what moves . . .

[Baba' interrupting] Sushumna is not a nadii. Within sushumna there are three nadiis. Sushumna means 'tube'. Within it there are three nadiis.

Q: What is the name of the first nadii, the innermost nadii? Brahma nadii.

Q: You said that what flows through this Brahma nadii are tammatras, a term which is generally used to refer to sensory inferences. You speak of this flow as being an inferential flow of tammatras, suggesting that perhaps the flow through the Brahma nadii is essentially an abstraction, that there is no actual presence of matter, subtle matter or even mind that is in movement. What do you use the word 'tanmatra for?

These are inferential flows of mind, not in association with physical objects but in latency, manifesting reactions to prior associations. So they are not responsive frequencies, but reactive frequencies, inferential flows of the mind. 'Tanmatra' is used because there is inference, inferential expression. Is it making sense? I think it is clear, so let me go on.

There is within the development of a human being a latent potentiality for the transmutation of consciousness. This latent potentiality lies coiled at the base of the spine. Coiled means it is sleeping but ready to spring. In the base the kundalini remains dormant. Mind has activated within the physical structure through the tonal waves according to prior samskaras, but it has not developed its full potentiality of expression. Expression is only in accordance with prior samskaras.

So what happens, due to certain experiences or spiritual practices there is the activation, the hammering if you will, upon certain nadiis, certain sub-glands or propensities, and so they begin to acquire strength and the flow of divine energy towards the Supreme gets activated. This creates a kind of suction within the sushumna, causing the kundalini to begin to rise. When it touches the chakra all of the propensities of the mind get affected, all of the petals within the vajra nadii begin to vibrate and they begin to turn upwards. They get a directional flow towards the Supreme, rather than a directional flow towards the diversity of physical expression. So they gain a kind of unison of vibration. All become purified or directionally focused. As the kundalini rises through the different chakras, all of the propensities of the mind become single pointed upon the Supreme goal. When the kundalini pierces into ajina chakra then the directional flows become united and the little mind merges with the Great.

But before this can happen, all of the propensities expressing various frequency variations which have come to constitute the samskaric development of a human mind must get unified in a singular direction. Before this can happen there must be a purification of body and mind. This requires Brahma sadhana. The practices of yama and niyama will also affect this mental development. When the petals, that is, propensities of mind or tonal frequencies, begin to resonate in a subtle flow, they begin to form a kind of unison of direction. When this upward movement of the petals occurs, the tonal frequencies begin to hum in a certain seed sound. This is biij mantra. When this seed sound is fully frequency harmonized, all of the propensities of that region will become directed and harmonious in their tonal vibratory rate and it is said that the petals will turn upwards. When the kundalini rises through a particular energy center resonating the petals and focusing them, the biij becomes vibrated and the entire center gets aligned. Then there is complete harmony in the subtle body.

When this occurs the nervous system is biochemically impacted. Biochemistry is altered, nervous system is altered, glands altered, the entire plexii and mandala become affected. There is a kind of resonance that develops which, like a stone dropped in a pond, goes out in ripples affecting the whole biophysical structure.

Then as this process continues chakra by chakra and the kundalini rises, the mind of a human being becomes transformed or transmuted and the direct experience of the Supreme Cognitive Entity becomes available to the human being. The human being finds that the qualities and characteristics of that Entity begin to manifest in their mental expression. The body becomes sweet and resonant, dominated by sentient principle.

When kundalini rises, different types of experiences may happen. For some people, there will be very little external phenomena. Kundalini will rise in a systematic fashion with very little extraneous activity. There will be very little kriya, or phenomenological experience. For others when the kundalini rises there will be resonant activation within the other nadiis, and there will be varying phenomenological experiences as these propensities begin to vibrate at a different rate. A person may have many subtle and pleasant experiences, they may manifest different types of kriyas and have so many different perceptions.

There are different ways in which the kundalini rises depending upon the samskaras of the individual, but it will always arise through the central most column. Those who say it is arising through citrani nadii or vajra nadii are incorrect. It will vibrate those nadiis in some people, so they may think it is rising through those nadiis. But this is an incorrect understanding. It only rises through Brahma nadii. In some people the other nadiis will vibrate, in others the rising will be very unobstructed and there will be little experience of vibration within the other nadiis.

Q: Could you explain what happens when kundalini is awakened, without clearing the path, by way of trauma, accident, childbirth, etc.?

This happens to people, oftentimes because in a past life the person has done Brahma sadhana but in this life the opportunity for sadhana has not as yet arisen, so the person may stumble into some experience. Due to past samskara and past development, kundalini may be already awakened from birth. When they come into the life kundalini may already be at a certain stage and they do not even know it. Then some experience happens which brings about awareness or activation of these forces which were developed in the past. Thus the person begins to have some dynamic experience of the rising of these energies within the body and mind. However, if the person's physical body is not properly developed there may be a psycho-physical disruption leading to mental or physical disturbances, or both. When a person has a guru, one who has knowledge of these matters, and is given a systematic approach – asanas, pranayama, sadhana, the practices of yama and niyama, – when a systematic approach is given to the person usually these traumatic difficulties will get resolved if the person follows strictly.

If the person should have the samskara from a previous life for spiritual development, but in this life has been eating meat and doing activities which crudify the mind and body, and then suddenly out of nowhere from their view these forces become activated, there is bound to be some disruption of psycho-physical parallelism. The person will require some guidance, some care, some systematic approach, even though many times they will not be able to follow good advice in the beginning. You will have to help them along step by step. Sit with them, meditate with them so they can use your strength for the sadhana. Give them asanas, give them mudras, give them certain pranayamas, depending upon the area in which the blockage is located.

When the entire psycho-physical structure has become redirected in a sudden way, and the physical body is not up to it, a gap develops between the subtle body development and tonal frequencies which are realigning and the physical nerves and glands which cannot go along. So you see why a problem develops. It can become quite serious. A person's entire physiology and biochemistry must be altered, and the person may be overcome with great fear for their physical safety. You think, "Kundalini, ah, it is beautiful; one sees Divine," but such people are very afraid. They may not experience the beauty of Parama Purusha because they are too busy noticing that everything they thought to be the basis of their existence is quite ephemeral.

Yoga Psychology

So for such people you will have to give them guidance. Not only will you have to give them good advice, you will have to sit with them, do sadhana with them, step by step help them along with particular types of assistance so that their biochemical physiological structure may become again aligned with their subtle body. Otherwise they can suffer greatly and even lose this expression.

Q: It is said that the kundalini is coiled three and half times counter-clockwise. What is the significance of the direction that kundalini takes?

You see, ida and pingala are based in the psychic development of a human being within the nuladhara chakra. They are, as I have said, directional flows. One will bring the mind to subtle mental forms, the other brings the mind towards the physical forms. They move outwards and diverge in different directions, and then they converge, they switch directional flows. Now the kundalini lies latent or dormant within nuladhara chakra, held in place by a 'granthi' or knot. It is a psychic knot which sits upon this center.

When ida and pingala arise they pierce this knot in their first directional movement. The coiled energies of kundalini are said to be three times coiled, that is, in the physical, mental and spiritual spheres, and the head, or the half time as it is referred to, lies in the granthi pushing upon it. It cannot spring unless the plug or block is removed. This is done by the activation of ida and the flow of mind into the subtle intellect. The best method for gaining this flow into subtle intellect is Brahma sadhana. Then in the physical, mental and spiritual spheres of the human expression, a movement may begin to unfold or unwind. When it is fully unwound it will be unwound through all three spheres.

This science may seem a bit technical, but it is very important to know, because knowing this one will understand the different states of mind and difficulties that a human being may encounter in the process of their sadhana. One will come, through knowledge of this science, to know how to adjust and move the mind in the proper directions in a systematic way. This is why I say the science of yoga is methodological. It is a complex and precise science.

[January 21, 1997]

Yoga Psychology

The Psychology of Yoga

Today's topic is again the psychology of yoga. Yesterday we spoke of the subtle body and its interaction with the physical body. Today I will focus upon the relationship of the subtle body to the mind. You know, when a human being is born, already the mind has attached itself to the physical structure. This happens while the fetus is still in the uterus or at the time of conception – it varies, depending upon the samskaras of the mind which is associated with that particular physical structure. At times the disembodied mind will stay closely associated but will not enter the physical structure until the time of birth. It depends upon the samskaras of that person.

Now when a person dies mind becomes disassociated from the physical structure. The vayus are withdrawn and the human being enters a kind of sleep in most cases. In this state there are no indriyas, no organs of perception in the physical world, and so mental existence, comprised of the bundle of samskaras, takes expression in the astral plane where mind begins to dream. Now the human being may dream many things, depending upon their samskaras, but what is significant is that this will be an internal experience within the mind. It will not find externalization in the physical world because there are no indriyas, no organs to receive or to perceive the physical world. Existence is contained in svarloka, not in bhurloka.

Yet the disembodied mind has a desire to express its

samskaras, and this mental expression will not suffice. Let us say there is a boy and he wants to go fishing, so he will in his mind dream of fishing. In his mind he will take the rod, he will throw the hook in the water and imagine he is fishing. But a time will come when he will become somewhat discontent with his pleasant dreams because he wants the actual physical experience of fishing.

So like this the mind, absorbed in its imaginative flow, becomes restless for physical expression. This may happen in a very short time or after many thousands of years. It depends upon the samskaras of the individual as well as the availability of a proper physical structure. So when the opportunity arises where there is a compatible physical form in which the samskaras of this mind may take manifestation, this urge to actualize the imaginative dreams in the physical world draws the mind back into association with another physical structure. At this time the disembodied mind will take association with the embryonic form, and in that association they will form a psychic link that is first through the manipura chakra.

When the mind enters the physical body, there is an activation of the subtle psychic body. In the disembodied form the human being has no expressive organs. The mind dreams and lives in an imaginative state. When it comes in association with a physical structure and enters that structure then the mind begins to take on a formation which is allowable within that physical structure. For example, if a human being, due to samskaras, enters the body of a frog, then that person will take on the requisite subtle vibratory frequencies that may be expressed in the physical structure of a frog. When the disembodied mind enters a human form, likewise, it will take on the requisite subtle structure which is capable of being expressed in the human body.

Now in the human form all of the faculties of mind are fully developed, so that there is within the human physical structure the capability for expression of all layers or facets of mind. A human being has the quality of self-reflection which is the most subtle mental capacity. When the disembodied mind which lies in an imaginative form comes in close association with a physical structure it will begin to align itself in parallelism with that structure and take formation according to the allotted subtle structure which may manifest within the potentialities of the physical structure. Thus the mind begins to align with the chakras and the propensities available in each of these centers. The requisite mental flows begin to gravitate towards the different chakras in accordance with the capacity of that center to express those mental tendencies.

Thus the mind becomes seated in the body. It becomes seated in all of the chakras and expresses through the fifty vrttis, or propensities in the first five chakras. Within ajina chakra, there is a directional control (para and apara). It will be activated with a different emphasis at different times and to varying degrees, depending on the past development of the individual. According to the development of a person during their life a different directional movement will be activated.

Now the point was brought regarding the human brain, which is seen as the controlling organ of the entire nervous system and the seat of the mind. In fact it is the seat of the mind in its most subtle form. It is the seat of consciousness and the seat of the Cosmic Mind as it associates with the physical structure. However, the human expression is seated not in the brain, but in the entire nervous system and glandular system. It is seated in the chakras. The brain is the controlling organ for the nervous system, but the subtle body is the controlling entity. Thus the human mind is embodied through the subtle body and expressed through the nervous system and the glands. Although the brain is a controlling organ, the mind lies not in the brain but in the subtle body. Brain does the activity, follows the instruction of the mind.

The human mind has many capacities and capabilities. It is a most complex and sophisticated expression. If there is damage to the brain, then this complex mental capability will not find expression in the physical world. The brain is the tool of mind which through the nervous system expresses in the organs and receives sensory input. The brain not only involves nerves, but biochemistry. Therefore the glandular system is the controlling system of brain function, for nerves are biochemically based. Without proper glandular secretions and biochemical secretions of the sub-glands within the nerve plexus, you will not have good brain function. Brain will be abnormal, even if nerves are physiologically intact. A cat scan may be taken and brain will look fine, but if nerves, glands and sub-glands are not secreting in a proper way the person will not be able to have a proper mental expression. So that is why it is said that the glands and sub-glands are the controllers, not the nervous system. Do you see?

Now, I was saying, mental development is very complex in a human being because a properly working human structure has the full capacity for complete psycho-spiritual expression. Not all who have acquired a human form utilize this capacity. Some live only the life of an animal in a human body. They eat, they procreate, they enjoy the sensual pleasures of the body, but they do not take advantage of the full potentiality of a human existence. This is a waste of a precious human life. The ability to attain a human body is somewhat rare. One should never waste this opportunity for full and complete development, for the capacities of a healthy human form are very great indeed. In a human body all of the capability is there for the development and expression of subtle psychic flows.

Human beings need not confine themselves, should not confine themselves, merely to physical pleasures, for the human potentiality includes the development of intellect and of self-reflection. A human being may think, "Who am I, and why have I come into this world?" This is the specialty of a human being, to reflect upon his or her very existence. Not only does a human being feel a full gamut of different sentiments, not only can a human being learn many facts and figures, but the human mind is capable of rationality, of analytic thinking. In its most refined state it is capable of analyzing the nature of its own existence. This is the special capacity of a human being.

You know, there are many variations in the human form. Not all look the same. In different regions the body may look different, the color of the skin may vary, some may be short, some very tall. Perhaps there are major differences in physiology, yet a human form has certain basic capabilities and that is what defines the human structure. So in a far distant part of the universe a human structure may be quite different, but it will have the same requisite capabilities. If those capabilities are not there, it is not a human form and because these capabilities have a certain frequency of expression you will find even across vast distances of this universe that there is some similarity of human form, though there will also be some differences.

Now the human mind is one which requires mental stimulation for its growth and development. It cannot develop properly in a vacuum. A human being, to be healthy, must grow with love and nurturance, with kindness and caring around them. They must have proper opportunity for their expression and encouragement for their development. They are not simply machines. For proper human development there must be proper circumstances otherwise the full capacity of the human being cannot express. When the mind becomes focused on the Supreme due to self-analyzation and self-reflection then a human being begins to have a sense of their own existence, they begin to activate expression of propensities which may have been dormant or undeveloped, and they begin to assert themselves in ways which their prior animal existences could not manifest. When this happens, transformation happens in the development of the human being. The mind becomes more developed than the body. Mental capacity, rationality, refined intellect grow. The person takes interest in the arts, in the sciences, in the more subtle and refined expressions of their existence. They begin to appreciate beauty, to enjoy listening to fine music, to enjoy reading high quality literature. A person with this type of intellect is reflecting the refinement of mental development.

As a human being grows not only is there refinement of mental development but in this mental development a self-reflective awareness begins. "I am enjoying all of these fine artistic endeavors but what is the meaning of my life? I have a fine intellect and I enjoy knowledge but who is it that enjoys the knowledge?" A person becomes self-reflective, and then the capacity for knowing the Great comes in hand. Self-reflection is the key with which to open the door to the Divinity that lies within.

The layers of a human mind, or 'koshas', are seated in the subtle body within the chakras. They take the assistance of the various elements in each chakra, and diversify into propensities or vrttis. The mind seated thus, expressing within the subtle body and activating the physical structure, is unit mind. But in the subtle structure associated with the physical structure of a human being lies the latent capacity for the activation of the channels to Cosmic Mind. Thus when the kundalini begins to uncoil, it moves mental stuff from the individual expression through the channels of the subtle body to activate more subtle propensities which propel the mind.

Do you know the sentiment of longing located in the vishuddha chakra? When this propensity becomes activated it creates a kind of vacuum or negative pressure which pulls the kundalini. At the base of the spine is the fundamental negativity, at the top is Parama Shiva, the fundamental positivity, and a kind of vacuum is created when these subtle propensities become truly activated. First there is mental development, refinement of the mind, and then there is the activation of the longing for the Great. This longing creates a kind of sucking or pulling, which creates the capacity of kundalini to unwind, to leave its base in the fundamental negativity and begin to make the journey towards the fundamental positivity or pure cognition; the pure, unattached, completely self-resplendent cognitive manifestation.

So consciousness is drawn from matter, through mind, to the abandonment of mind in a pure cognitive stance. In this process many changes and different experiences may happen for a human being. The journey from the stance of fundamental negativity to fundamental positivity is a journey from consciousness in association with the material world, through the transmutation of mind into more and more subtle spheres, until unit mind becomes so expanded in the causal layers that it cannot maintain its individuality. That individuality then becomes dispersed like a drop of water falling into the sea, and the individual mind becomes dissolved within the Cosmic Mind.

The kundalini will rise up in different patterns according to the samskaric blockages or barriers which the particular individual mind is configured in. It may rise progressively, it may rise and fall. There are different patterns. When the rising occurs, as I have said, there is an activation of the petals or frequencies of expression around a given chakra and they begin to hum in harmony. That harmony or sympathetic vibration is pictured as petals turned upwards. There is a harmony of frequency and alignment as they withdraw into the seed biij, and then all of this harmonious vibration becomes focused and rises upward. But in some individuals, if there is one particular attachment or the vayus are not completely in alignment, there may be some different reactions, some different kriyas as the physical body and the sub-glands adjust to the alteration in frequency.

So different types of experiences will happen for different people. If the body is very pure, the nervous system pure, able to handle these alterations in the subtle system and their altered relationship with the physical structure, then there will be no symptoms at all.

Consciousness will just rise into the pure effulgent blessedness of union with the Supreme. But it is a bit rare that a human being will have no difficulties at all with parallelism. There are normally some sensations in the spine, some varying kriyas, some different types of experiences and in some people some difficulties also may arise as this psycho-physical adjustment occurs. That is why there are asanas. They should be done so that these types of problems do not arise, that psycho-physical parallelism may be maintained. There are other practices which will work upon the elements and purify the citrani nadii. This is very helpful for the purification of the frequencies in each center. Now I will take questions.

Q: In Ananda Sutram it is said that death is a long sleep in the causal mind and is described as being like a dream. How is the mind able to function in svarloka, to have even dream-like experience, without a physical form?

The mind dissociated from the physical body first is drawn to a more subtle sphere. But most, unable to maintain parallelism with the causal cognitive flow of the Supreme Entity, are drawn by the latent passions within the mind into the various realms of svarloka where mind internally reproduces its desires much like a person dreams. No physical organ is necessary for expression in this loka because there is no physical manifestation. It is an internalized psychic flow, a kind of recreation of psychic images which are moved by the mental propulsion of latent reactions. No new samskaras are created in this state nor are those mental reactions fulfilled for they must gather a kind of momentum which drives them again into the physical realm where they find expression in a more solid way and fulfillment. But this is a good point. The mind does get drawn into the causal sphere but for most parallelism cannot be maintained due to the drag of the reactive samskaras which have an association with physicality and pull the mind closer and closer to the physical world. Do you understand?

Q: Does a person maintaining mental activities in svarloka require a subtle body or receptacle?

No, because it is not mental activity which expresses. It is contained within the mental field of unit mind. It is a kind of internal dreaming. The mental field of the reactive potentialities is a kind of field in which there is play, but I would not call it a receptacle.

Q: Can a disembodied mind communicate with a physically embodied entity?

On occasion one who is disembodied may come in association with one who is embodied in the physical world. There are no ghosts who will light a fire in your home or move objects around a house. There is no capacity for one in a purely mental expression to do these things but on occasion, due to the intensity of their desires, or due to the intensity of the desire of one in physical form – either way or both – they may come in contact with the mind of an embodied entity and find mental expression within that mind.

So you will see that many wives, when their husbands die, will have communication with their husbands and vice versa. It is not uncommon and why is this? Because both the wife and the husband have strong attachment, very strong attachment to each other. So when the one leaves the body the other calls to them, "Come to me, come to me; I miss you". The one who has left is very worried for the one who has stayed. This worry draws their mental momenta close to the mental sphere of the embodied individual and they may take mental expression within the mind of that person, but they still cannot act in the world. The physically embodied person may pick up an object or use their telekinetic ability to move an object. The disembodied person has no such capacity. It is only through the capacity of an embodied person that this may occur. So there may be some contact like this if the desires are very strong between the two.

Q: There seems to be a greater occurrence now of people having a partnership with disembodied entities for the purpose of helping or counseling others. Is this a similar process of communication?

There are as many different processes as there are different types of beings in this universe. You know, this is not only a physical universe. It is a multidimensional universe, and so there are many types of beings who take residence in different lokas. Though there may be similarities there also may be differences, because one cannot compare the expressions of one who is manifesting existence in svarloka with one who is manifesting existence in maharloka. The expressions vary a great deal as to what is occurring, but the question has been brought, "Is there more of this?" I would say there is, because of the needs of this planet at this time. It is a critical time in human history, and so there is more guidance from others in different subtle spheres of existence than there has been in the past. This is due to the opening of certain channels or avenues.

The subtlety of human beings is growing, and as it grows human beings become more capable of receiving guidance from the intuitional flows of the Cosmic Mind and from subtle entities who manifest in other spheres. There are not only those beings who are ripening their samskaras in svarloka, but there are those who have developed extensively and have taken upon themselves bodies of light, bodies of microvita, and these beings appear to human beings from time to time – more now due to the needs of this planet and the opening of channels of light which have grown stronger as the astrological formations have altered. Also, the guidance of the cosmic cognitive flow is finding manifestation and form at this time so that the human race will not destroy itself. It is a critical time in human development.

Q: Are there practices that we should do to increase our access to these higher sources of guidance?

There are. First of all, you should know that your Guru is always with you, that you are never apart, and your separation is only due to the barriers of the mind because of its association with physicality. Mind is malleable. If you dream always of the physical world the mind will go the physical world; if you dream of Parama Purusha mind will go to Parama Purusha. It is the way of human mind.

If you want to have Guru, if you want to know Guru's guidance within yourself, you must direct your mind to him. Not here and there, not one half hour each day, but day and night, night and day, no matter what you do, see him in everyone, see him in everything, look only to Guru, feel only Guru, see only Guru, be only with Guru. And hear his voice in every voice, hear his song in every song, see him in every eyes, see him in every heart, feel him in every experience – both pleasurable and painful. And with all your mind, with all your heart, with all your being, love, love, love. Then when you sit to meditate and you go to Guru, ask him with your heart, ask him with your mind, ask him with all of your being to please come to you, to please be with you, and surely he cannot refuse. The shower of his grace is then bound to fall upon you. If there is something he would want you to know, when you open yourself thus you will know it, if it is in words, if it is in pure knowledge which dawns in your mind. If you go thus to him, if you see him thus all around, when he speaks you will know. Whether his speech is in word, in light, in knowledge, you will know. Many are his languages.

Q: When I try to conceive of existence in svarloka, it seems a kind of purgatory in which the mind is confined for a long period to experience a lack of purposeful expression.

It is a sleep state, the mind is asleep. But, you know, when the mind is first drawn from the body, it is pulled out and goes to the light or to the causal realm where it becomes suspended in function. You see, its function in the physical world is suspended. Mind is asleep in that it cannot express in the physical world, there are no organs. But its reactive momentum is not. It is held in suspension with regard to actual expression, but it exists. It has existence, and it is pulled towards the physical world by the samskaras desiring physical expression. If these samskaras for physical expression are very minimal and mind requires some subtler expression, it will find the embodiment in microvita, or even in the pure cosmic light. But if the desire for physical expression, for physical development and outlet is strong, then the mind will get gravitated closer and closer to the physical plane until the match is there.

The cosmic arena is a vast cosmological web in which the entire manifest universe is woven, and a living being is threaded through this tapestry in a most beautiful way. There is no purgatory. The mind is merely churning, churning, and the churning becomes more defined as it comes closer to finding physical expression. Now, if there is pain in a human being it may be relieved and even resolved in this sphere. I would not call it purgatory. It is merely a state of latency in which the mind is suspended. Is it clear?

Q: So is there a kind of active ideation, or is there only the playing out of past desires?

What is mind apart from the physical structure? There is in mind an accumulation of repulsions and attractions, reactions to past actions, repulsions and attractions, fears and desires. It is an accumulation of fears and desires surrounding a central locus of "I" feeling. So these fears and desires, attractions and repulsions, swirling around a central sentiment of "I exist", this is mind. When it leaves the physical structure, does it cease to exist? No, it continues to exist. It has no vehicle for expression when it is denied physical structure – unless mind is more attached to subtle interests, in which case this locus of "I" feeling and its attractions and repulsions will get a requisite body in which those subtle feelings may be expressed. But otherwise it will return to the physical world. And in that time between it remains dormant from the physical world. But it still exits. There is still the sense of "I" feeling, of "I exist", and surrounding the "I"-ness is the swirl of attraction and repulsion. It is not a purgatory. It is merely a disembodied state from the physical realm.

Q: Would you encourage us to try open channels to entities in other realms and to receive information from them?

I would not encourage random opening to other psychic entities. You are all sadhakas; you must come to know Parama Purusha. There are so many beings in this universe. Some are very benevolent, some are not so benevolent to human beings; some have very compassionate motives and some do not. Each of you has the capacity to open to this type of communication should you desire it, but I would not recommend such pursuits. They are irrelevant. What guidance you need, you seek from Parama Purusha. You seek it in your sadhana and surely Guru will be there to guide you. Don't go to anyone else. It is not required, for you have Guru. You do not need Seth or Emmanuel or any of these beings. They may be very good. You may read what is written and feel inspired. If it inspires you, very good, very good. But you do not need these beings for you have Guru. Go to Guru within yourself and take his hands and walk home with him. You need nothing else.

Q: Can you explain a little more about the forms of the piitas in the citrani nadii of each chakra? Are they actual forms, like square, crescent moon, etc. or are they a kind of energetic formation?

These are representative configurations. When you visualize a square, a triangle, a crescent moon, in that visualization is the essence of the quality. The color and the form are an essential symbolism which attempts to express the vibratory frequency of that element. In the same way, you say the biij mantra which also attempts to express the frequency of the element. So with the physical voice you attempt to imitate the tonal frequency of the element, or the configuration with the biij mantra, and with the visualization the mind attempts to form a vibratory compatibility. So through visual and auditory senses mind attempts to emulate the vibratory frequencies of the fundamental element as it is manifest in citrani nadii. But this is not the biij sound itself, because the biij sound is not physical. This is only the vocalization of the sound.

If you do certain types of sadhana you will hear the sounds emanating but still what you hear in the mind is not the sound itself. For the sound itself is in the subtle body, and it is not a physical sound. It comes to the mental body as a mental sound, and then it may be said with the mind, formed in a mantram which emulates that subtle vibratory frequency. The visual pattern also is the same: it is an emulation.

[January 22, 1997]

Transformation of Consciousness and Mind

This morning I will discuss yoga psychology and how it relates to the different states of mind that a human being might attain. When a mind enters a human body it manifests itself through tonal frequencies which emanate throughout the subtle system into the physical body where it is then regulated by glandular secretions and biochemical development. Then it is expressed through the nervous system and the organs of perception and expression. Thus through the organs the mind comes in contact with the physical world, expresses samskaras, and receives new information and new experiences. It also develops new samskaras.

Within the subtle body the mind has found emanation in the subtle tonal waves. These are not audible to the ear. Any sounds that are audible to the ear are imitations of these subtle tonal frequencies. They can be heard deep in the mind. They are the expressive waves or vibratory frequencies through which mind comes into existence. They say that in a human being the last sense to be disassociated is what? It is hearing, it is sound, is it not? Because sound is the most closely associated sensory experience to the mind, the mind disengaging from the physical sphere will disengage in the tonal sphere last. It will remain in the tonal expression the longest.

Now in yoga psychology it is said that a human

43

mind is the product of collected samskaras expressed through the varying layers of mental development (koshas), all of which may be manifested in human experience. Now these layers of mental development, or koshas, are linked with the elements, the energy centers (or piitas) and the biija sounds. Different strata of human expression will be associated with different chakras and different elements, different biija sounds. So these strata of human mental expression have this correlated association.

Now in the subtle realm the mind of a human being is manifest in a variety of levels or strata. These strata each have specific characteristics and qualities, which I think you may read about in the philosophy. Each one is associated with specific mental functions, but each one also has the capability of transmuting into a different type of experience. As the kundalini rises through the sushumna the layers of the mind recede one into the next, so that the conscious mind recedes into the subconscious strata and those stratums recede into the unconscious. Thus the conscious mind becomes aware, not of material existence but of that which lies in the unconscious and that which is causal in nature.

This cannot happen until the layer of samskaras (reactive momentum or psychic tendencies) becomes suspended. When an individual goes into various samadhi states the samskaras become temporarily suspended. That is, the reactive mental tendencies of the mind, which cause the mind to stray into the various vrttis, become suspended.

Mind withdraws from externalization into the vrttis, the petals of the chakras turn upward, and the human mind is suspended in a directional flow towards the Supreme.

When this occurs there are several distinct alterations in the psychic flow of a human being. Mind begins to flow inward towards the nucleus, rather than outwards towards the sensory organs. As mind flows inward towards the nucleus, the conscious mind which has been so busy - buying groceries, cleaning the house, talking to friends - so busy in these activities of the sensory organs, becomes withdrawn from the sensory organs. Mind begins to focus inward upon its own nature and its essential composition, which is cognition.

So mind reverses its extroversial flow into an introversial pattern and the conscious mind begins to experience an internal pull. The samskaras of the human being are temporary suspended. They become calm, quiet. The urge to express becomes still. Then the urge to move in the internalized flow becomes so intense, so sincere, that the externalized tendency is dissolved. The human mind flows into more and more subtle states of awareness. The conscious mind becomes disassociated from sensory organs, disassociated from psychological states and various tumultuous sentiments within the mind. It moves beyond the first and second layers of the mind and begins to move into the causal mind, or the unconscious. There the mental tendencies are very directed.

In this process the mind goes from a concentrated

state to a meditative state, a state of dhyana where the mind flows freely. It is just in a flow. There is no tendency of the mind to revert externally. All thoughts or mental images that come are in the stream of this internalized flow. Then as this stream becomes more and more concentrated, the mind begins to enter a trance state, a state of intense absorption we call samadhi. There are many stages within this. As this occurs, there is suspension of all extroversive tendencies for a brief period. However, due to the latent tendencies which are merely suspended, not resolved, after some time the mind begins to again feel the urge to express. So the mental tendencies which are merely pacified for a short time begin again to awaken and express the urge for association with the extroversion of mind into the sensory organs. As the mind begins to reform the old psychic tendencies that it is patterned to express, the samadhi state diminishes and the human being finds they are as they were.

If it has been a particularly profound experience there may be some fundamental changes and the person may notice they are not quite as they were, but, in the main, the mind again returns to its original state of functioning. The person's particular psychic tendencies and mental distortions again become expressed.

This process does not go on for long before there begins to be a fundamental alteration in the very structure of the human mind. The person will find that they are somehow a bit different than they were, that exposure to these states of inordinate absorption has somehow fundamentally changed their basic psychic structure. Their mental tendencies and desires begin to change and their modes of expressing begins to alter. It is not that the person says, "Oh, I am now convinced. I am going to the Himalayas and I will follow all of these rules and I will be a good person." This may happen, but this is not the change I am speaking of. This is not a contrived change; this is a fundamental change, fundamental to the internal psychic structure of the individual.

Within them the psychic structure begins to alter due to close association with the Supreme. There is a fundamental change in their internal nature, and overdue time that begins to reflect in their external expression of self. As they continue to have exposure to the sweet and loving presence of the Supreme Entity, they begin to emulate that Entity in their existence. As they continue to experience the expansion of self into a cosmological association with the Divine Entity, they find that there is a fundamental change in how they view themselves, in how they know themselves and how they know others. Who they are in the world becomes different. They become very close to that Supreme Entity and so their expression in the world becomes sweet, reflecting his qualities and characteristics.

As the sadhaka continues their sadhana and the kundalini continues to rise above anahata chakra, the changes in their psychic expression become even more profound. When kundalini begins to remain above anahata chakra in a stable way, the human being develops the capacity for love. They feel that they are in love with every living being. They feel that they are one with all beings. They become a neohumanist.

When the kundalini rises beyond anahata chakra to vishuddha, then the human being gains a pinnacled intellect. They feel that this entire universe is the manifestation of the Divine, and they do not draw distinctions between themselves and others. When the kundalini rises through vishuddha chakra and pierces ajina chakra, then the human being finds a permanent dissolution of their sense of individuality. The little "I", the little person, gets dissolved in the big "I", in the Cosmic "I". This is the attainment of mukti. It can be done by a human being in a single lifetime if they are sincere. This is the potentiality of the human mind. All of the practices of Brahma sadhana and the knowledge of biophysiology are directed to this end.

But, you know, even in this state consciousness is still bound. It is bound in Cosmic Mind. Only when moksha is attained does consciousness become unbound. Then it is not associated with any media other than itself. It becomes unbound from mind and returns to its original state of complete equanimity. A human being cannot live in a human body in this state. They may experience nirvikalpa samadhi and be entranced in the state for many days but beyond 21 days the physical structure will die. So a human being must return to the physical structure and to mental function if they are to live in a human body. One who has crossed this boundary will never be the same.

To enable a human being to reach this pinnacle of human existence there must be a systematic approach for the transformation of consciousness. Otherwise, this lofty goal may become very difficult indeed to achieve and some people, not having proper guidance and a proper system, may even find some serious difficulty as their consciousness moves and transforms. So one will have to have a proper practice of sadhana which systematically removes the mind from its extroversial tendencies and draws it through the layers of mental expression, through the sense of doership which pulls the mind to express in the world, and finally into the sense of "I"-ness, or the mahat. For in that "I" lies the key to the doorway.

So there will need to be a systematic approach to sadhana plus a system to keep the chakras nicely balanced and keep the nadiis opened. In addition there needs to be proper care for the physical body: a system of aerobic exercise, of yoga postures and of cleaning of the body, proper fasting for internal cleanliness, and proper bathing for external cleanliness. All of this is required to maintain a sweet and sentient vibration which will allow the mind to move towards the Supreme. One must have a complete system, including pranayama, to balance, purify and concentrate the mind.

It is not good to teach forms of sadhana that are incomplete. You give a person just a visualization and you say, "Do this." That is good and well but when one wants to realize the Supreme, when one wants to break the bondages of individuality, there must be a systematic approach which takes care for body, for mind and for spirit. Otherwise a person may become highly imbalanced. There is a history in India of many great saints, great yogis who would go into the forest and do sadhana for long periods. They would ignore the needs of their physical body, and what happened to these people? They may have attained very high states of spiritual awareness, but they could not bring those states into the world. They could not become an asset to society as they should because they did not balance the mental, physical and spiritual states. So they were not an asset to the society, or perhaps they were an asset in that they were very high yogis. Perhaps they had enough mental function that a few wise words would come from their mouth. So the people came and they gave a few wise words and this is good. At least they were giving something but they may have misguide those people because they had no system to offer them. They have no systematic approach.

So how are people to develop themselves? How are they to learn to be balanced in the world, to be able to be physically strong and healthy, to be able to be mentally fit and in peak condition and to be spiritually deep and sound? Those people who are fully developed in all spheres will make the greatest contribution to human society. And that is the goal of sadhana, to have complete balance. Do you understand? So you see, there must be balance. If a person is very good in the physical sphere, but without sadhana has cut from themselves so much of their human potential, it is a tragedy. Likewise those intellectuals who teach, who move around in the universities, in intellectual settings, who are scientific and contribute in the mental sphere to human society, may give great contributions to society, but if they themselves have ignored their physical development or they have ignored their spiritual development, again it is a tragedy.

One cannot ignore any of these areas and grow to the maximum of human potential. All areas must be given good attention. Not everyone will be an athlete. I do not mean to say that you must be some sort of athletic person. If you have that capacity in your physical form, that is very nice and you should keep it toned and developed. If the physical form that you have is not that of an athlete, still it should get proper exercise, it should get sentient food, and it should properly rest. You must maintain balance in all spheres. Between your work in the world and your internal time for your personal development there must also be balance. This way you will become an all-around, optimal human being. This human life will have maximum positive development, and you will become an asset to the human society.

You know, yoga means "union". You may even drop the word if you do not like. If it is not fitting to your language, use another but the goal will be one of all around development for the union of the little and the Great. So be

Yoga Psychology

vigilant in your teaching that you do not ignore any area of development. Be vigilant in your personal development that you do not ignore any area. You set an example of balance for others. That way equanimity will come in the mind, peace and harmony will be yours. You will learn to see the Infinite in all that surrounds you, to dissolve all that is extroversial into the pure introversial flow to the Supreme, and in the ocean of love, surrender your being. This is a pinnacled human life. I ask each of you to lead such a life.

[January 27, 1997]

Glands and Sub-glands

There are in the human body subtle glands, or propensities which control or regulate the human psyche. They are not physical, but they are correlated to the physical body. You see, the word "gland" is a translation. It means hormonal secretion which regulates or controls different mental states. So each propensity of the human mind is associated with particular biochemical states, and there is regulation of these states. There are fifty of these sub-glands in the human body, but they are not physical glands. They are different biochemical formations. They are associated with the endocrine system, with the glandular system and the hormonal secretions of the body. In the physical body this involves the entire endocrine system and it also involves the central nervous system and the different types of chemicals produced in the brain and in the nervous system. There is a complex and involved biochemical process which correlates to the formation of the different vrttis or propensities of the human mind.

So there is a potential for many types of expression – fifty different directions of expression and the combination of those directions. This potential lies within the biochemistry of the human body and is regulated by the glandular system. The production of different brain chemistries and neurological transmitters is also involved but the key is that all of this is governed by the endocrine system and is very much influenced by the condition of the glands.

The sub-glands are not physical glands in the human body, but are sub-categories of secretions which are formed from the glandular secretions, or which are influenced by the glandular secretions. For example, the pituitary gland will influence many different secretions in the body. If there is a lack in pituitary function, there may be a lack in growth hormone. There may be a lack in other functions within the body, the metabolism may not be correct. The expressions of the human mind within a physical structure are dominated by the capacities of that structure. The entity inhabiting the body may only have expression in so far as that structure is capable of providing the expression.

The human body is capable of providing the expression of fifty different directions and the combinations of those directions. This is done through the development of the endocrine system and the influence it has upon the biochemistry of the brain and the nervous system. So if the pituitary functions one way, there will be one tendency, and if it functions another, there will be another tendency. If the glands are not strong or healthy, different diseases may occur and different mental states will be affected. All of these glands and hormonal secretions must be balanced so that the chemistries of the brain and nervous system are also balanced.

The term sub gland refers not to physical glands, but to the biological impact of certain glandular secretions. It represents the different biochemistries which effect mental states. So controlling the pituitary gland, the thymus, the gonads, all of the glands, will make a difference in the state of mind of the yogi. If these glands are brought under conscious control then the very chemistry of the brain may be influenced. As the kundalini rises up the spine piercing the different centers, it alters the biochemistry within the nervous system. As this happens, all of the glands and sub-glands get directed, and all of the propensities of the mind are directed to a single focus. This is because, as these different glands are aligned, their function is brought under the control of the pineal gland, and then the functions of the brain are also influenced. Different types of chemicals are produced within the brain stem, within the brain itself, and certain areas of the brain are stimulated. Then the kundalini will rise up the spinal column and into the brain itself making a permanent alteration in consciousness.

So the term sub-glands should not be interpreted literally to imply there are undiscovered glands. But it also should not be taken metaphorically as a symbolic point, for it is quite literal and relates to biochemistry.

[October 12, 1995]

Yoga Psychology

Nadiis

Nadiis are pranic energy channels. Pranendriya controls the flow of this prana throughout the body. The subtle body, the mental body which is linked to the physical body through the chakras and expressed through the vrttis, or propensities of mind, is controlled by the glands and sub-glands and also associated with prana. Pranendriya regulates the expression of mind. Mind is expressed through the mental propensities, which are controlled by the glands and sub-glands. The physical glands are regulated by pranendriya. The rhythm of the physical and mental body and the interface of these two is regulated by pranendriya. Mind is regulated by pranendriya.

Now the nadiis are the channels for prana within the body, which pranendriya regulates. There are different pranas in the body which flow thorough the channels or nadiis. Pranendriya regulates the flows of these different pranas which regulates the expression of mind.

So mind flows through these pranas into the material universe. Then the glands become affected and develop in certain ways because the pranic flows have established a pattern which reflects the samskaras. The samskaras manifest as the propensities (vrttis), the configurations of mind, the signature of the mind which has come into the body. Then the glands and sub-glands, biochemical configurations of pranic flows, will regulate the expression of the mind. Mind will come with a certain pattern. That pattern will establish the different flows in the nadiis and the regulatory system. These will be regulated by pranendriya. Pranendriya will then regulate the glandular development. Glandular development will reflect the mental development and the nervous system will develop according, biochemistry will develop accordingly, and samskara will become reflected and expressed in the physical universe.

[February 20, 1997]

Vrttis of Vishuddha Chakra

Q: If the vrttis are mental propensities, how can the first nine vrttis of vishuddha chakra (the seven sounds of animals or the musical scale, the sound of kundalini and the "om" sound) be identified as a form of mental expression? What practical examples can be given for expression of these nine vrttis?

These nine vrttis are not propensities in the sense you are thinking. Each chakra sustains the mind in a different way. The vrttis are not in the same stratum, therefore, their expression and development differ. The lower five chakras are within the cosmic citta, however they span the lokas, thus they differ in how they operate. The propensities emanating from the different chakras will have their roots or origin in different stratums of cosmic expression and therefore their roots within the human mind will be different.

The root of vishuddha chakra lies in the realm of potentiality, or maharloka. Therefore, it is an expression of the subtle potentialities of the human mind. It does not have its root in bhurloka (the physical world), though these subtle potentialities may in fact emanate through all the spheres and find expression in the physical world. It's root lies in maharloka. Do you understand?

So the root is different, therefore the description is difficult. That is why animal sounds are attributed. When the root comes to its expressed form in the mundane world,

59

it will take a sound similar to the animal voice. It will emanate that vibration and carry the essence or origin of that form of expression. But in the vishuddha chakra it lies in the realm of expressed potentiality. It is neither fixed nor differentiated. So these sounds that will occur in the manifest world as expressions of the human mind are the waves or potentiality of each of these creatures. Do you understand?

The wave of potentiality of the expression of each of these creatures lies within the human mind. The sound, or the vibratory frequency of their essential origin, is a characteristic of the human mind and lies within the potentiality of human expression. It takes manifestation often in the voice of lovely singers who may intonate these subtle vibrations of vishuddha chakra. For you must remember this is the sphere of potentiality. In this sphere the human mind has its most subtle expression. It is a sequence of tonal waves resonating with great refinement and these tonal waves are the very expression of the human mind. When taken to complete extroversion, they will vibrate the resonance of each of these creatures. The qualities and characteristics of each creature are a part of the human potential, a part of the human expression. That does not mean these qualities or characteristic expressions are of the animal mind, but that they contain within them all of these expressions of the animal world, or the essence of these creatures and this essence is expressed in vishuddha chakra as tonal waves.

When a person is gifted with access to these propensities, the voice becomes musical and the manifestations of the animal kingdom, that is to say the expressions into flesh of the subtle realm, become intonated in lovely tones. For the essence of all beings, the essential origin of all creatures, is sweet and lovely beyond comparison. When this beauty becomes expressed in the voice of a great singer, you will feel sweetness, you will feel the loveliness of each tonal origin and you will enjoy very much. These are the subtlest expressions of the human mind.

When they are crudified and enter into bhurloka, they take the form of the various animals or their mental equivalent. So the person who has, for example, given expression to the tonal potentiality known as sadaja in the mundane world, will have the pride of a peacock and the air of that animal. They will express it in their human body, but it is a characteristic that one will recognize if one observes the peacock. Likewise, if the sadhaka or human being becomes dominated by the ray of rishabha or the bull, they will have a very bullish nature. It will dominate their overall expression because it comes from the most subtle sphere. Do you see? Each of these creates an overall approach.

If a person is dominated by one alone, they will have the very quality of that creature. So if you meet someone and they are bullish in nature, if you watch them and then you watch the bull, you will notice the similarity. Then you will know they are dominated by this propensity. In its pure form, it is a sweet and subtle tonal wave, a potentiality of the human spirit and sweet beyond comparison as the essence of all beings is sweet. But expressed in a dominant way, in the life of a human being, you will notice that all of the propensities of that mind fit into this bullish character. Like this they dominate the human mind, if they are in excess.

The same may be said for gandahara, or the tone of the goat. You will see the person who is dominated by this propensity. Observe them, they will be like the goat. In whatever they do, whatever they express, their expression will have a goat-like quality. They may like to climb rocks or to eat anything in sight. Then they may "baa" at you if you say something. But in the subtle form, in the essence, this characteristic is also sweet, for all beings are lovely in their essence. If there is a mix of these different potentialities of expression, if each of the propensities have some degree of activation but none is dominant, you will get a more complex expression. The person will not resemble a particular animal in their manifestation or overall development but you will see hints of many creatures in them, of many influences on them.

Now as to "om" and "hum", I have said that vishuddha chakra lies in maharloka so that in vishuddha chakra the very roots of creation exist and are manifested in the "om" sound. This is the realm of potentialities. In this realm time, place and person are indistinct and the creative energies of the universe find their first expression. This emanation of creation is manifest in the mind of the human being. It is one of the propensities of the human mind to create because it is the propensity of the cosmic progenitor and you are but His reflection, Her reflection. So the "om" sound manifests this propensity and if a person becomes dominated by the ray of this propensity or expression within the mind, there will be all manner of creative expression.

You will find such people are highly creative. They will become artists of note, they will become great scientists because they are immersed or dominated by the propensity for creativity. They will express great potential for the development of new activities, new ideas. They will be innovators, creators in whatever their mind is directed towards. Wherever their focus is placed, new ideas, new ways of doing will pop in their mind. They cannot help but create. These people have a dominance of this propensity and in the mundane world it takes such a form. But if they do sadhana, and they look to the subtle internal realms and come to the origins of this propensity in vishuddha chakra, they will discover that their little "I" is not the creator and that all the universe is being created every moment within the mind of the cosmic progenitor. They will experience the bliss of His infinite creativity. So you see how this propensity manifests in the human mind and has its origin in the expression of Parama Purusha in maharloka.

Now the "hum" sound, or vibratory wave expressed

in vishuddha chakra, is the manifestation of the subtle waves that vibrate and form in the vishuddha chakra. This is the acoustic root of this chakra. It is also an emanation or propensity in that this wave, this subtle expression, has scope in human expression, and that scope is expressed as an intense longing for the Supreme. That is the expression of this propensity. When it dominates the human mind, the person will be mad to know God. They will think of nothing else, day and night. They will long for Him, they will cry for Him, they will want nothing but Lord. One who is dominated by this propensity will not seek mundane knowledge, but knowledge of the great. They will feel the kundalini in vishuddha chakra. This chakra will open for them and all of the subtleties of this sphere will dominate their mind. In the mundane world they will be religious or a spiritually minded individual who will have a tendency to always seek holy places, to look at the sunset and think of God, to search for spiritual knowledge and to seem a bit otherworldly. You will notice such people. You see these propensities of vishuddha chakra give overall direction to the life of a person. All of the other propensities of the mind from the lower chakras below this stage will fall in line with these more subtle leanings. So if a person, dominated by the wave or ray of "hum" should be in the world and experience fear, they will fear that they cannot find God. If the bullish person has a fear, it will be that they are not sufficiently powerful.

So you see, these propensities of vishuddha chakra

direct the other propensities or expressions below them. Many people will not be dominated by one ray alone, but three or four will mix together. So it is often not so black and white to see what propensities dominate.

[August 29, 1996]

Awakening Kundalini Safely

The kundalini resides in the nuladhara chakra. It is the storage place of the individuality which is expressed in this created universe. The kundalini must rise upward through the chakras or energy centers within the body if the consciousness of a person is to change from the small consciousness contained within the activities in the mundane world to the pure self-awareness of the infinite Purusha. For this transformation, the kundalini must be awakened. When the kundalini becomes awakened, it begins to traverse the journey upwards through the spinal column toward the apex of consciousness.

You know, this journey can have some hazards if it is not properly guided. There are those for whom, by dint of sadhana, or perhaps by the reactive momenta of past samskaras, the kundalini will awaken somewhat spontaneously. It may be in any circumstance. It may be while walking down the street, it may be while in a particularly intimate context, or it may be in deep meditation. When this happens, an individual might experience some rushing of energies up the spine. They may feel the waves of energy moving upward through the spinal column, they may experience some waves of bliss accompanying this.

When the kundalini rises spontaneously it may be somewhat of a shocking experience for the body and for the mind of the individual. They may or may not have some acquaintance with these characteristic experiences, so it may take them by surprise. If they are unprepared, if they have no guidance whatsoever, no one to say, "Eat this food, eat that food, do not do this activity, do this and that, keep a moral life, do the yoga postures." If they have no one to guide them like this, then it may be that they may experience some unusual sensations, some difficulties as the kundalini opens and rises. There may become mental block, some physical blockage, some psychic blockage. There may be some impediments, and so some unusual experiences, not always pleasant, may occur.

It has been said, "Guru Brahma, Guru Vishnu, Guru Devo Maheshvara": the Guru is the creator, the Guru is the preserver, the Guru is the destroyer of all that exists. If a person would engage in raising the kundalini, then it is very wise for that person to have some guidance and who should guide that person? Should it be anyone whatsoever? I do not think so. Should it be anyone who has studied and who considers themselves an expert? I do not think so.

Who should guide a person having this experience? It should be one who has, first of all, knowledge of the path, and who has raised the kundalini force within themselves to its apex. The one who guides should have practical experience as well as knowledge that comes from teachings and texts. They must have practical experience. So this is the first qualification that must be there for the one who would guide. The second qualification is that the person guiding this movement of the kundalini must not be expressing themselves in limited consciousness. They must be expressing the Brahmic flow only.

You see, there is only one Guru. Is it not? There is one Guru, one supreme, infinite consciousness which is quiescent in this entire manifest universe. The consciousness which lays quiescent in all existence is the Guru. It is the creator, the preserver, and the destroyer. This consciousness underlies all manifest expression. So, who may guide the upward movement of the kundalini? Only that consciousness that infinite, omnipresent, omniscient consciousness may guide. The words of guidance must come from that Omniscient Entity, and through the five fundamental factors that Omniscient Entity may give the guidance in the physical world. The guidance for this process cannot come from any lower source, otherwise it is the blind man leading the blind man, is it not? The blind cannot lead the blind. Only one whose eyes are open may lead the blind. So the guidance must come from the Guru when it comes to the upward movement of the kundalini.

If a person should experience this movement without a Guru, it may be somewhat difficult. It may be somewhat hazardous even. There must be, at some point, the contact with Guru. Guru may come in physical form, Guru may come in internal form within the mind, but Guru must be contacted or else there is bound to be serious difficulty over time.

How may a person contact Guru? How may a person come in the proximity of that omnipresent,

69

omnipotent entity who is manifest in the sahasrara chakra and who is the controller of this entire manifest universe? How may a person come in the contact of that entity? You know, when an individual becomes one pointed in their ideation, when, through whatever circumstance, they come to desire the Infinite, that desire alone is a potent force. The desire may carry a person beyond the limitations of their ordinary mind. Due to this desire to know the Infinite, they say, "Oh Lord, I must know you. I must have you as my own." Through this desire a person may come to the place where they come in contact with the Guru, where Guru's grace may come to them.

Guru may appear in the subtle form to them, or Guru may take the form of a spiritual guide, a physical person to show them the way home to their own self. When the mind becomes concentrated, it comes within the sphere of the Divine Entity. The desire draws one to that Divine Being. Now there are certain practices which may be beneficial: the practice of meditation upon the Great, the practice of following an ethical code (the yama and niyama), the practice of purification of the body through asanas (yoga postures), the proper care of the physical structure, and the pursuit of knowledge of the Great. All of these things are beneficial and assist one to come in contact with the Guru and to raise the kundalini in a balanced fashion.

However, there is one other practice which is far superior to any of these practices when it comes to propelling the mind forwards to the Divine and that is the practice of love and devotion. When one begins to love the Divine, when the heart, soul and feelings are opened to Divinity, then true progress will be made. You know, this love for God is not easily acquired. It is not automatic. Through good works, through ideation upon the Great, through studies of the qualities and characteristics of the Great, one may come in contact with the Infinite and in that contact one may experience the blessedness of the Divine Entity.

In that experience, there comes the awakening of the heart and the soul and the individual says, "Oh Lord, I had no idea what I was missing. I did not know how beautiful you were. I did not know how exquisite it is to experience you. I was thinking that pleasure was from the objects that surround me. I did not know what pleasure truly is. I did not know what joy truly is. But now that I have touched you, I see the world is bland by comparison to you my Lord." When this experience comes in one form or another a living being will begin to develop devotion. They will put their feet on the path of bhakti or love for the infinite.

When this happens, they find they are in a relationship to the Great. You know, you have one relationship to your husband, to your wife, to your son, your daughter; you have these relationships, do you not? But those relationships are somewhat limited. You may love the person, they may love you, but there are certain boundaries that must be adhered to because you are both temporal entities. The passage of time will change the relationship. But Parama Purusha is not a temporal entity. He is an infinite Entity beyond the scope of time. So when you have a relationship with that Entity, that relationship transcends the scope of time, transcends all the finite boundaries of this manifest universe.

When an individual enters into a relationship with the Infinite, they begin a divine dance, a divine drama which is ever unfolding and which will ultimately lead to a most sweet and sublime contact with the Infinite Expression. So when the feet are placed on the path of devotion, the being thinks, "Oh Lord, you are exquisite beyond belief. My heart is enraptured. I can think of nothing but you. I have wanted many things in my life, but now I see they were small and irrelevant compared to you. My Lord, all my passion is to know you, to love you, to be very close to You."

When this happens, what is He to do? What can He do when this impassioned plea is made by the devotee? The Lord is not heartless. When such attraction is there, that Infinite Entity must come in further contact with that individual. So the Infinite will find one form or another to express His grace in the world for the pleasure of the individual entity. The Infinite will come and show His multifaceted supreme expression to the person who has this enchantment and thus the enchantment and devotion will grow. The purer the devotion is the more the Divine Entity will reveal Himself, and the kundalini will naturally rise in the proper channel. There will be no difficulty, none at all.

All of these problems, all of these difficulties will get resolved. They are due to lack of contact with the Supreme Guru.

Once Guru is there, Guru will take the loving devotee in His arms and He will carry him or her forward, carry him or her through. So there need be no further concern. In the path of love, in the sentiment of devotion, the feeling comes "I will give everything," because the vision of the Great is in the mind. The feeling comes. "I will give everything. I will surrender my all to the Infinite Guru who has come in my vision." So, in the path of devotion, the individual surrenders their preconceptions, their passions and desires, their mental function, their life itself at the altar of the Infinite and having given all to that Entity, what do they have? That Infinite Consciousness will accept the gift, and in return the person will find they have come in close contact with the Infinite Expression. They will no longer feel that they are separate. The fundamental cause of their suffering will be resolved and the kundalini will have uncoiled fully and risen without any difficulty.

So for those who are serious about spiritual life or who have inadvertently experienced the awakening of the life force energy latent at the base of the spine, it is wise to seek the shelter of a knowledgeable person and the guidance of the Supreme Guru. For only when contact is made with the ultimate positivity which is the Guru residing in the sahasrara chakra can the force of kundalini get proper direction. A journey undertaken without a clear direction can become troublesome. For a successful journey to be undertaken, for the life force to arise and go straight to its goal, one must understand the goal. One must have at least a nominal perception of one's destination, then the path will unfold. In Tantra there must be a Guru, a knowledgeable guide, and proper practices to ensure that the path of blessedness will not be accidentally missed.

[September 29, 1994]

Vrttis and Spiritual Development

Today I will speak about the relationship between spiritual development and the vrttis or propensities of the human mind. You know, within a human being there are certain configurations of mental tendencies which become manifest in human life. First of all, there are those propensities which are involved in the basic survival of a human being, that are seeking shelter and food for the basic subsistence of physical existence. Then there are those propensities which have to do with procreation and those which have to do with the emotional development of a human being: pride, lust, fear, all of these are also there. There are other propensities as well; the desire to realize the Great, the subtle desires in the human mind, the desires for knowledge, so many desires.

These propensities, or vrttis, are multilayered, existing within the different layers of the mind but all of these propensities serve one purpose. They serve to manifest the experience of a human being. The desires perpetuate the physical, mental, psychic and emotional existence and expression of human life. So, they are the outward projections of human existence.

Now, these propensities combine in various forms to formulate the behavior patterns and expressions of a particular human being. It is a fact that anyone who inhabits a human body also acquires these propensities, because they are a part and parcel of the humanoid structure. So,

75

when a human being becomes attracted to the Great, these propensities of the mind become focused and directed toward the Great. The propensities which help to increase one's attachment to the Supreme will become larger and more dominant and those propensities which draw the mind toward diversity will begin to become less and less dominant. Eventually, as the sadhaka (spiritual aspirant) continues in the practice of sadhana, all the propensities will have less and less influence on their development and psychic expression. That expression will, instead, become dominated by the extroversial flow of the Supreme Being, not by the individual samskaras of the particular person.

So you see, what a person thinks, what a person does, how they respond, is all dictated by the extroversial flow as expressed through the psychic propensities of the mind. The governing force for those propensities may be the desires of the little, individualized ego or may be the flow of cosmic awareness. Whatever the governing entity, the media for expression are the fifty propensities of the human mind, or vrttis. These constitute the waves upon which the desires, latent within the mind, can find expression in the manifest world.

Thus, individualized expression occurs through the vehicle of a human body and a human mind. Cosmic Mind may also express through the same vehicle. In that instance, it is not the individualized samskaras laying latent within the unit mind which govern what combinations of propensities dominate the mind and get mental expression.

It is instead the Cosmic Mind which dictates what propensities dominate the psyche and what expression occurs. So you see, the vehicle is one and the same but that which is expressed through the vehicle may differ from person to person, from one time to another time.

There is a key formula if the individual would give expression to forces aligned with the Cosmic Mind. They will have to give up their individuality and, instead, identify with the Cosmic Mind and with the awareness which underlies the expression of Cosmic Mind. When this identification with Cosmic Mind is made, what expresses through the propensities of the human mind will not be merely the samskaras or latent reactions of the particular person, but the expressed flow of the Cosmic Entity. So you see, it is possible that a human being may not only express their individualistic desires through the vrttis of the mind, but also the will of the Cosmic Entity, the harmonious centrifugal flow of the Cosmic Mind.

So the propensities of a human mind are neither good nor bad. They are merely the characteristic expressions available to a being in humanoid form. From whence they are governed makes the significant difference in how they configure to form psychic expression and for what intention and results actions are taken. It is very significant that the results of actions expressing cosmic feelings do not create samskara. They go to the Infinite Entity, to the Cosmic Mind, not to the perpetuation of a sense of separate individual existence. Only those actions taken with the little feeling of separate existence are the cause of accumulation of latent reactions. These reactions cling to an individual sense of existence, so that 'I, mę and mine' grow stronger and identification with the Cosmic Mind and Awareness are dimmed in the consciousness of an individual.

The more these reactive momenta are accumulated around a sense of individuality, the stronger the sense of separate existence becomes. The pleasures and the ultimate pain which this brings accumulate and accumulate until one day it is so extreme that the living being must search beyond a limited sense of individuality. On that day they will be blessed with the grace of the Supreme Purusha and Cosmic Awareness will dawn in their mind. The door out of suffering will open for them and they will see the bright dawn of spiritual light in their life. This is the blessing of the Cosmic Progenitor.

So do not judge lest ye be judged. Do not covet lest others covet what you may have. Do not steal lest others steal from you, and finally, do not separate yourself from others. For you are not a little being. You are not a small person. You are not a body or a mind. These are your vehicles. You are the One, Supreme Consciousness, manifesting in a multitude of forms, sizes and shapes. This body and this mind are only one of a myriad of forms which you find expression in. So know that you are not a petty ego, you are not a separate, isolated entity. You are forever One with all life, forever One without a second. Identify yourself with this Cosmic unity and break the bondage of deluded thinking which causes you to identify with a separate, isolated expression. Break the bondage which causes the arousal of the feeling of I', me' and mine'. This fundamental identification with the little is the basic cause of all suffering.

So if you would bid an end to suffering, if you would withdraw the mind from the battering of attraction and repulsion, you will have to withdraw the mind from the feelings of I' and mine', the feelings which define one's existence apart from all else. You will have to withdraw the mind from these feelings and from the sense of separate existence. You will know you are not a little body, you are not a little mind; you are not a separate being. You will know that you are melted into the essential nature of this cosmic projection. You are in all manifest expression and you are also in unmanifest expression. You have always existed, and you will ever exist, changeless. Though you undergo innumerable changes, you remain changeless, dancing the infinite dance of the cosmos in all the multiple colors of this universe. You are changeless, eternal, undisturbed by the play of opposites because you have no sense of separate existence. Instead you feel 'I exist everywhere in all things and my nature is love itself. My nature is beyond polarity. I am self-resplendent'. Thinking like this, the very cause of suffering becomes annihilated.

What is the cause of suffering? The cause is the basic sense of separate existence, and from that, the feeling of 'I', 'me' and 'mine' as opposed to that which is not of me. So the feeling of 'I exist everywhere' will help one to avoid that which will diminish one's existence. Break this chain of suffering, break it where it is most vulnerable, where is can be broken. Break the identification with separateness and then surely you will come to feel the wholeness which is your birthright, your identification with that which is pure and changeless, your essential nature.

[January 4, 1995]

Brain Waves and Tonal Waves

Q: Is there any particular wavelength that can be described for every chakra, i.e. alpha, beta and theta waves?

You are speaking here of brain waves. Each chakra is dominate by tonal waves. The propensities are tonal waves not brain waves. It is more subtle. All of the manifest universe is composed of subtle sounds, not brain waves. But, the brain may express the propensities of the human mind. It is designed, along with the nervous system of the human body, to express the spectrum of frequencies available to the human mind. In this expression of the spectrum of frequency available to the human mind, and emanating through the chakras in the petals or rays of manifestation, the human brain will employ all of these brain waves. You see, if a person will gain the frequency, or subtlety of the emanation of vishuddha chakra, they will have to manifest a like biochemical and electrical expression.

The brain will produce certain chemical and electrical responses. In subtle manifestation there will be the dominance of theta and delta waves in the brain but when the same propensities are expressed in the mundane world, they will use alpha and beta as well. The man may create in a deep alpha state, but express that creation in words utilizing beta waves. Different biochemical processes will be initiated in the brain.

81

Yoga Psychology

So all of these electrical and biochemical processes of the human brain and nervous system are designed to express each of these subtle or crude propensities. Depending in what sphere they are expressed, different biochemical and electrical responses will be there. Is it clear? It is not that the expressions of nuladhara chakra require beta or other chakras theta. No, no, no. It is not like this. It depends on whether the root is involved or if it is expressed in the mundane world using the voice and words in the mind. Do you understand? This is not the association between body and subtle body. It works in a different way. The physical body will use all of its capacity to express the vrttis of the human mind.

[August 29, 1996]

Subtle Sounds and Language

Human beings came to vocalize approximations of the subtle sounds emanating from the different lotus petals, or directional flows of energy regulated through the chakra system, by the development of language. These subtle emanations become the guideposts for the manifestation or expression of human existence. So it is through their influence that a human being has the configuration of expressions available to them.

Matter flows from subtle spheres. When the energy crudifies, it materializes forming the human body. When the subtle sound crudifies, it materializes in the form of audio sound. So you see, the subtle becomes crudified into the material world. Likewise the emanations or tonal frequencies which constitute the range of experience available to a human being become crudified and manifest in external sound. Then these sounds are combined to form languages and these languages become the crude mode of communication in the auditory sphere among human beings. In the psychic sphere language is also used, but it is more precise. The same tonal frequencies or ranges are available to human beings in the psychic sphere, but the sound is subtle, not crude. So you see, this is the nature of human manifestation.

Certain people who have done considerable exploration into the subtle realms have been able to analyze this system and to codify and classify these sounds into certain categories. They have been able to develop a systematic understanding of the energy fields of the tonal waves and the resultant areas of dominance. Thus the chakra system has been outlined and the science of sound explored in the subtle realms. From this has come an understanding of how the subtle sounds crudify as they degrade into physical sound and how they impact different chakras. These subtle scientists discovered that there is an entire science to this and that certain glands or propensities might be controlled by the use of certain sounds, both subtle and crude. From this has come the science of mantrum. It is an exacting science, and in this age experts in this field are very rare, but the basic knowledge has been handed down through the ages. It is a science known to older races who have studied these matters and to human beings who have walked the inner realms.

Sanskrit came from an earlier language. This language was a developed language because this science of sound was actively used and considered in the development of the language. The knowledge that this scientifically developed language is based upon comes from those who have studied the subtle science of sound. They have outlined the basic tonal categories. In this early language, tonal alterations were used a great deal to make an impact upon the mind and body so that many things were communicated through tonal variations. It was a very musical language and one in which tonal combinations could be used to communicate subtle feelings and nuances that are difficult to express in most modern languages. That is why I say it was a developed language. The range of expression of subtle emotions was much greater because tonal sequences were very sophisticated and attuned to scientific understanding of the tonal structure and nature of the human experience.

[January 28, 1996]

Subtle Sounds and Colors

Sound and color vibrations both exist within a living being who has form in the world. There is a color or a hue to every mind and a tonal frequency which is the combination of all of the frequencies used by that mind. When all of these frequencies of a particular mind are combined to give the personal signature, if you will, of an individual, then we may say that they have a particular hue or color. So each living being will have a particular color in the world and a particular sound.

You know, these are not physical colors, they are not physical sounds. They may be seen as colors, they be heard as sounds, but it is a particular vibratory rate. It is only when it touches the organs of perception that it becomes color or sound. It is seen visually, heard auditorialy, experienced in space or in touch depending upon the sensory organs of the receiver of the tammatras.

So this is interpretation due to sensory definition. The tammatras which are sent - whether they be heard, seen or felt are the same. Depending on the sensory complement and emphasis of the individual receiving the tammatras, they will experience color or sound. But really it is a frequency that is being emitted, a tonal signature, if you will. If it is sound, if it is color, that comes from the sensory organs, not from the manifestation. The manifestation is a particular wave length that is occurring. That wavelength

Yoga Psychology

will have many interpretations depending upon the vehicle which is receiving it.

[December 28, 1995]

Glossary

AJINA CHAKRA   Third eye, the controlling chakra of the lower five chakras, the seat of cosmic mind.

ASTRAL   Svaraloka. Cosmic realm of mental or ephemeral existence.

ASANAS   Yogic postures performed for physical health and mental balance.

BRAHMA   Supreme Entity.

BHAKTI   devotion, love for God

BHURLOKA   A layer of Macrocosmic mind associated with the physical world.

BIIJ   The seed. Essential vibratory tones of the five elements.

CHAKRA   Psychic energy center.

CITTA   Screen of the mind in which experience is played out. Objective part of the mind.

CITRANI NADII   A subtle cylindrical channel between Brahma nadii and Vajra nadii within sushumna.

FIVE FUNDAMENTAL FACTORS   Etherial, aerial, luminous. Liquid and solid, expressed in

Cosmic Citta due to increasing pressure of the operative principle or Prakrti.

GURU   One who dispels darkness and guides towards the light.

GRANTHI   Knot or blockage. Sanskrit for gland.

IDA   The channel or nadii influencing psycho-spiritual flows. It pierces sushumna at each chakra and exits through the left nostril.

KUNDALINI   'Kula' means coiled or latent, 'kundalini' means serpent power or universal energy. When at the muladhara chakra or base of the spine kundalini is said to lay in potential like a coiled serpent and is thus called 'kundalini' or coiled serpent.

KRIYA   Phenomenological experience (sounds, movements, tears, laughter, etc.) as the result of resonant activation within the nadiis.

KOSHA   A layer of individual mind.

LOKA   A layer or sphere of the macrocosmic Mind.

MAHESHVARA   The destroyer of illusions. An aspect of Brahma.

MANDALA   A larger area than the chakra, it includes plexii, nerves and glands and interfaces the physical and subtle bodies.

MICROVITA   Fundamental units of life force.

NULADHARA CHAKRA   Psychic center located at the base of the spine.

MUDRA   Subtle hatha yoga practices for improving health and assisting the mind to be ready to meditate, also gesture used in dance.

MUKTI   The permanent merger of unit mind into the cosmic mind, Saguna Brahma. The spiritual aspirant has become established in the cosmic "I".

MOKSHA   The permanent merger of unit consciousness into unqualified Consciousness, Nirguna Brahma. It is the state of total suspension of both individual and cosmic mind.

MANTRA Sound which liberates the mind; used in meditation.

NADII Subtle channel through which prana flows

NIYAMA   Behavioral observances of yoga.

NIRVIKALPA SAMADHI State of total absorption in Cosmic Consciousness, with complete suspension of both cosmic and unit mind.

PURUSHA   Cosmic Consciousness.

PRANA   Vital energy. PRANA (pl)

PLEXUS - PLEXII (pl.)   The psycho-physical interface between the nervous system and the subtle tonal frequencies.

PROPENSITY   Mental Tendency, Vrtti

PRANIC   Vital energy.

PRANAYAMA   Practices for of control of breath.

PARAMA PURUSHA   Supreme Consciousness.

PARAMA SHIVA   Supreme Divine Consciousness.

PIITA   A seat, controlling point of the five fundamental factors in citrani nadii. Seat of the organ (linked with the citta).

PINGALA   The subtle channel influencing physical energy. It pierces sushumna at the chakras and exits at the right nostril.

PRANENDRIYA   Controlling center of the ten vayus. Psychic organ situated in the area of anahata chakra (yogic heart).

SUB-GLANDS   Activated mental tendencies (vrttis) through which the pranic force flows. Biochemical formations which correlate to the different vrttis or mental tendencies. They involve the biochemistry of the nervous system and are controlled by the endocrine system. Not glands in the physical body.

SUSHUMNA   The channel or tube through which kundalini rises. It contains the chakras as well as Brahma, citrani and vajra nadiis.

SAMSKARA Potential reaction to a psychic action.

SAMSKARIC TENDENCIES Tendencies of mind (vrttis).

SADHANA   Spiritual practice; meditation.

SHIVA   Divine consciousness. Historical: Sadguru, founder of Tantra.

SVARLOKA A layer of Macrocosmic Mind; the subtle mental world. Samskaras exist in this loka.

SAMADHI   State of absorption, trance.

TANMATRA Minutest quantity or fraction of 'that', of the fundamental factors; supersensible inference or generic essence; tan (that) + matra (minutest quantity).

VAYUS   Vital airs of the body

VISHNU   The preservation aspect of Brahma.

VISHUDDHA CHAKRA   Psychic center or chakra located at the throat.

VAJRA NADII Outermost of the three nadiis in sushumna.

VRTII   Propensity, tendency of the mind.

YAMA   Behavioral abstinences of yoga.

About the Author and the Origin of These Writings

Maetreyii Ma, Megan Nolan Ph.D. has been a devotee of Shrii Shrii Anandamurti, who is affectionately called "Baba", since her initiation into yogic practices in 1969. A year after initiation she began to experience a blissful state, or Bhava[1] as it is called, in which she experienced Baba' manifesting in subtle form, conveying knowledge on many topics. She experienced a deep and compassionate flow of unconditional love emanating from this subtle manifestation of the Divine Guru (Ishta Deva) and was told that it existed so that someday she could learn to love others as he has loved her.

The years passed, and when her Guru, Shrii Shrii Anandamurti, left his physical body in 1990, Maetreyii Ma, through a series of profound mystical experiences, received direction from this Divine Guru within to begin sharing with others the deep and sweet guidance he had for so long been giving to her. Thus began the public expression of his intuitive Bhava emanating from this manifestation of Baba', the Divine Beloved.

Maetreyii Ma is a former director of the Spiritual Emergence Network, a founding member of the Kundalini

---

[1] A Bhava is a state of Divine love and inner knowledge - a mood of ecstasy, self-surrender, and channeling of emotional energies that is brought about by the development of devotion to one's Ishta Deva (object of devotion).

Research Network, founder and past president of Ananda Seva Mission, and former co-director of the Ananda Seva Yoga Teacher Trainings and Yoga Therapy Trainings.

Dr. Nolan is currently the president of Ananda Guru Kula, a non-profit dedicated to spreading the wisdom teachings of Yoga and a transpersonal psychologist in private practice. She spends her time giving 'Baba Talks', teaching and making books of these beautiful discourses. She is a wife and mother of two wonderful sons and currently lives with her husband in their ashram community in the Northern San Francisco Bay area.

Made in the USA
Middletown, DE
04 March 2024